Original title:
The Whispering Leaves

Copyright © 2025 Creative Arts Management OÜ
All rights reserved.

Author: Kieran Blackwood
ISBN HARDBACK: 978-1-80581-927-1
ISBN PAPERBACK: 978-1-80581-454-2
ISBN EBOOK: 978-1-80581-927-1

Green Symphony

In the trees, the breezes play,

Squirrels dance and glide away.

A leaf sings with a funny tune,

While ants march like a cartoon.

When shadows stretch, the laughter grows,

Frogs in coats strike silly poses.

A gust brings giggles from the pines,

As nature's orchestra reclines.

Ancient Echoes

Old branches creak, with tales to share,

As critters pause to stop and stare.

The mossy rocks chuckle in delight,

While owls hoot jokes in the moonlight.

An ancient oak, with droopy limbs,

Tells why the worm forgot his hymns.

The vines twist up for a sneaky spree,

As shadows tease, 'Come play with me!'

Sighs of the Wilderness

In the underbrush, whispers bloom,

While bushes giggle, filling the room.

A rabbit tumbles, a bit too spry,

His floppy ears just seem to fly.

A dandelion shouts, 'Catch me please!',

While the wind stirs up a breeze.

With each soft rustle, laughter swells,

And nature spins her quirky spells.

Secrets of the Canopy

High above, a parrot cracks a joke,

While hiding beneath, a shy mouse spoke.

The branches wiggle, what a sight,

As squirrels plan their next big flight.

From leafy nooks, secrets unfold,

With stories that never get old.

A whispering breeze, a playful tease,

As nature giggles with such ease.

Messages in Maple and Oak

Amidst the branches, squirrels play,
They send their tweets in a nutty way.
Acorns drop like secret notes,
While birds chuckle in feathered coats.

The maples dance with a creaky sound,
Their laughter spreads all around.
Leaves giggle as they twist and twirl,
With whispers of gossip that twirl and swirl.

Hidden Stories in the Underbrush

Ants march in lines, so very neat,
Sharing tales of their tasty treat.
A beetle boasts of a daring flight,
While grasshoppers jump, full of delight.

Mice scurry fast with tiny gabs,
Trading tales and a few fun jabs.
In the brush, where stories bloom,
Creating laughter, dispelling gloom.

Breezy Secrets Shared

The wind whispers as it breezes by,
Telling secrets with a whoosh and a sigh.
A rustling rumor that tickles the ear,
While feathered friends giggle, full of cheer.

With a gust of wind, one leaf takes flight,
In pursuit of laughter, oh what a sight!
It tumbles and spins, in a playful dance,
Inviting all foliage to join in a prance.

Murmuring in the Dappled Light

In sunlight's glow, the shadows play,
Whispers and chuckles come out to sway.
A dappled dance of light and shade,
Bugs crack jokes that never fade.

Beneath the boughs, where shadows scheme,
Leaves chuckle softly at a silly dream.
With each rustle, a giggle so sweet,
Turning the forest into a comedy seat.

Secrets Carried on the Wind

In the forest, secrets fly,
Squirrels plotting, oh my,
A turtle in its shell, quite wise,
Grinning at the birds' surprise.

Frogs croak jokes without delay,
While flowers dance in bright ballet,
Bumblebees buzz in comical glee,
As the breeze giggles past the tree.

Old oak trees with limbs like thumbs,
Join in on the laughter, hums,
Rabbits hop with silly flair,
Chasing clouds without a care.

Serene Shadows

In shadows where the sun won't peek,
A raccoon fears her cheeky streak,
Mice play tag and squeak a tune,
Hiding from a grumpy raccoon.

A shadow flickers, who's that there?
An old gnome with messy hair!
He chuckles as he hides behind,
Silly antics, he's quite blind.

The leaves above start to conspire,
Sharing giggles, oh, they're dire,
The ground squirrels look quite perplexed,
As nature's joy, they feel so vexed.

Whispers Under the Canopy

Beneath the leafy, joking dome,
Creatures gather, far from home,
Chit-chatting 'bout wildflower trends,
Making bets on bunnies' bends.

A wise old owl gives a hoot,
With visions of a dancing root,
While fireflies flicker, play their show,
Swapping tales of midnight glow.

Among the ferns, a lizard prances,
While dragonflies twist in their dances,
Raccoons raiding picnics near,
As laughter floats within the sphere.

Hidden Harmonies

In the glen where giggles grow,
Tones of nature start to flow,
Frogs with flutes and crickets sing,
A harmony that makes hearts spring.

The rustling leaves join in the choir,
Mixing sounds, oh, how they inspire,
An acorn drops, a thud so loud,
As the chipmunks cheer, so proud.

Caterpillars dance with grace,
In this secret, leafy place,
A melody of fun and fate,
Nature's jesters won't be late.

Rustling Secrets

The trees are gossiping, oh what a sight,
A squirrel claims he saw a deer in flight.
Mistaken identity, or just plain nuts?
Nature's comedy, where logic cuts.

Leaves chime in, 'Did you hear that joke?'
A snail laughs slowly, with a tiny poke.
In the forest theater, laughter rings,
Who knew that the wood could have such zing?

Beneath the Canopy's Breath

Under branches, shadows dance so spry,
An acorn tells a tale to a nearby fly.
'Did you know,' it squeaks, 'I could be a tree?'
The fly just chuckles, 'Not if I fly free!'

The branches shake with laughs, it's quite the show,
As a wise old owl hoots, 'Let the fun flow!'
Each rustle and giggle, a nature's spree,
It's hard to be serious under such glee!

Conversations in the Breeze

A light gust carries whispers from afar,
"What's with the peacock? He thinks he's a star!"
The daisies chuckle, their petals in bloom,
"Oh please, yesterday he strutted in the room!"

Chirping crickets join, it's quite the chat,
"Have you seen those frogs? They wear the strangest hats!"
Each wind-swept giggle brings joy to the scene,
How nature thrives on comical sheen!

Nature's Softest Murmurs

In the meadow, whispers float like fine lace,
A rabbit quips, "I'm late for the race!"
The daisies reply, "We'll just take our time,
A slow stroll's better than a hurried climb!"

Breezy banter makes the flowers sway,
'Did you see that bee? He's buzzing with play!'
Under the sky, laughter's the theme,
Nature's softest giggles, a joyful dream!

Where the Earth Breathes Softly

In a forest where trees wear hats,
Squirrels hold parties with fuzzy cats.
They share acorns and dance with flair,
While birds gossip softly in cool, crisp air.

Frogs in tuxedos jump on the scene,
Bouncing around like they're on a screen.
They tell jokes that make flowers bloom,
As butterflies chuckle, spreading their gloom.

A raccoon sings opera, quite out of tune,
While fireflies twinkle, a shining maroon.
The ants form a line, marching with pride,
While a snail takes a selfie, enjoying the ride.

Laughter erupts, mixing in the air,
As the wind carries secrets, a charming affair.
In this playful land, where the earth does breathe,
Nature's quirks weave joy, just take a leaf.

Nature's Hidden Dialogues

Under the canopy, a debate goes on,
The flowers argue who's the fairest one.
Mr. Tomato says he's the best red,
While Lady Daisy rolls her eyes, feeling misled.

The bees buzz tales of where they've been,
Discussing the sweetness of every scene.
A ladybug chimes in, with a wink and a grin,
Saying, 'Your nectar days are ready to begin!'

The trees nod wisely, roots tangled tight,
Sharing old stories of their proud height.
The wind chuckles softly, swirling around,
Saying, 'Keep it down, or I'll blow you to the ground!'

And so there they gather, all lively and merry,
In nature's own forum, no need to be wary.
With laughter and chatter, they fill up the space,
These hidden dialogues, a fun-loving race.

A Symphony of Sibilance

In the meadow, the hiss of the breeze,
Conducts a symphony that climbs the trees.
Grasshoppers play their tiny guitars,
As crickets tap dance under the stars.

Owls are the critics, perched high and proud,
Offering opinions, but never too loud.
A concert of sounds, some sharp and some sweet,
With the rustling of leaves giving rhythm a beat.

When the sun dips low, fireflies join in,
An orchestra glowing, a luminous win.
The frogs croak a tune that's catchy and bright,
Making every creature dance through the night.

And as night falls, a new chorus takes flight,
Chirps and whispers in the pale moonlight.
In this lively meadow, the music won't cease,
A wacky ensemble of nature's own peace.

Echoing Dreams in Green

In the green realm where dreams take a stroll,
A playful rabbit is digging a hole.
His friend the fox teases, 'What's there to see?'
As they hop through the tall grass, wild and free.

A turtle rolls by, quite in disbelief,
Claiming he saw a magnificent thief.
Turns out it's just a rogue sock on the run,
Caught in the wind, oh isn't that fun?

The butterflies swirl, in a chaotic race,
Trying to catch up, but they lose their pace.
With giggles and whispers, they pause to unwind,
Creating a spectacle, one of a kind.

Where dreams echo loudly, and laughter's the key,
Nature's own playground, a sight to see.
In this world so vibrant, both silly and keen,
Each moment a treasure filled with fun and green.

The Softest Dialogues

In the woods where secrets hide,
Branches chat, they laugh and bide.
Squirrels gossip, acorns fall,
Nature's jesters, one and all.

A rabbit bursts, a comical sight,
Dodging shadows, jumping light.
The birds retell their day's affair,
As rustling grass joins in the flair.

Rain drops join the happy crew,
Tapping softly, oh what a view!
Caterpillars snicker all around,
In this jesting, leafy ground.

Whispers travel on the breeze,
Tickling branches, making pleas.
Dancing shadows play their part,
In this nature's stand-up art.

Nature's Quiet Refrain

Trees hum softly, what a tune,
Breezy laughter, afternoon.
A chipmunk's joke, a chuckle here,
Nature's giggles, loud and clear.

Leaves canoodle in the sun,
Chasing rumors, oh what fun!
Bees buzz by with tales so grand,
A comedy show, quite unplanned.

Blades of grass sway with a grin,
Twisting tales of where they've been.
The sky looks down with twinkling eyes,
Nature's comedy, in disguise.

Mice in boots, they dance around,
Sharing stories, silly sounds.
Underneath this leafy dome,
Laughter echoes, feels like home.

Underneath the Boughs

Under branches, shadows play,
Whispers shared in a goofy way.
The apples giggle, just like me,
As nuts drop down, a comical spree.

Frogs croak jokes from their wet throne,
A playful king, all alone.
Amidst the thicket, crickets sigh,
With squeaky notes that seem to fly.

Sneaky foxes hide with flair,
Plotting pranks without a care.
The bushes rustle, laughter spills,
Filling the air with silly thrills.

Beneath the boughs, the world's alive,
In this realm, jesters thrive.
With every flutter, every sound,
Nature's humor, laughter found.

Muffled Dreams

In quiet corners, dreams may creep,
Leaves are laughing, no need to weep.
A badger snores, a funny sight,
Muffled giggles throughout the night.

Stars up high, they twinkle bright,
Join in whispering, pure delight.
Clouds tease trees, a friendly game,
Jokes float up, it's never the same.

Silly shadows chase the moon,
Bouncing softly, an ancient tune.
Teasing fireflies blink and flick,
While crickets tell tales, oh so quick.

Underneath the starry dome,
Nature's stand-up, far from home.
With every rustle, each embrace,
A funny dream time holds its place.

Murmurs in the Breeze

In the garden, squirrels plot,
Chasing shadows, on the spot.
While the daisies giggle light,
Secrets shared from day to night.

Branches doubt their own height,
As the butterflies take flight.
With a rustle, leaves agree,
"Who ate all the acorns?"—me!

Rusty swings let out a creak,
"Is that a cat? No, it's a geek!"
Each green tongue has tales to tell,
Nutty jokes cast a leafy spell.

As the sunset takes a bow,
Winded tales we weave somehow.
Among the trees, mirth and glee,
Laughter whispers, "Come and see!"

Songs of the Forgotten Trees

Old oaks croon a soulful tune,
To the waltzing sun and moon.
"Why did the sapling cross the lane?
To show off its new cane!"

Maples tap their bark in beat,
"Who's got better roots? On feet!"
With a chuckle, pines swayed low,
"Stand tall, but don't steal the show!"

During storms they share their woes,
"Caught my hat! Oh, how it goes!"
But in the warmth, their laughter rings,
"Dance with us, oh, leafy kings!"

In the twilight, secrets fly,
"Did you hear that?"—an aviary sigh.
Nature's choir, in jest they tease,
Footloose tunes among the trees.

Fluttering Confessions

Little fairies play hide and seek,
Hiding truths with every peek.
"Did you know about the frog?
He thinks he's an opera dog!"

Wings flap with a boisterous cheer,
"Tell me what's buzzing near!"
As the petals sway and bend,
"Someone's giggling, let's pretend!"

Crickets chirp with witty rhymes,
"Who's the best at jester climes?"
Breezes laugh, soft pranks unfold,
"Is that a frog or tales retold?"

Rustling tales through dappled gloom,
Tokens shared in nature's room.
Under moonlight, secrets weave,
Fluttering truths the night will leave.

Dance of the Sylvan Spirits

Woodland spirits spin around,
In a whirlwind, go to ground.
"Did you hear that acorn's prank?
It filled the pond! Oh what a tank!"

Elves trust branches to catch their hops,
While tree trunks dance, and laughter pops.
"Who needs shoes?" they chant in glee,
"Barefoot feels just right, you see!"

Amidst tall ferns and mossy chairs,
Frogs conduct the merry airs.
"Be careful of that sly woodpecker!
He's the funniest neck wrecker!"

As starlight drizzles soft and clear,
Joyous spirits draw us near.
In this wild, whimsical trance,
Join the frolic, take a chance!

Stories in the Stillness

In the garden, a squirrel prances,
With acorns tucked in funny pants.
A snail shouts, "I'm racing!" What a sight,
But he's just slow, like a comfy night.

The flowers giggle in the sweet warm breeze,
Telling tales to the buzzing bees.
A ladybug winks with a tiny grin,
While ants march on, insisting they win.

Beneath the branches, a rabbit chats,
About all the adventures with the hats.
The breeze laughs softly, shaking the trees,
As they join in on nature's little tease.

Even the clouds join in the fun,
Drawing mustaches till day is done.
With every stir, there's laughter and glee,
In this stillness, we find joy, you see!

The Language of Nature

Oh, look at the tree trying to dance,
With limbs that flail, giving it a chance.
The wind whispers jokes that only it knows,
As the bark nods in laughter, striking poses.

A chipmunk decided to bust a move,
With tiny spins that are quite the groove.
While shadows giggle and twirl with grace,
Nature's own disco, an endless embrace.

The bushes chatter about the best food,
While the daisies sway in a playful mood.
A rabbit trips over a clover patch,
But laughs it off, planning his next catch.

In this language where chuckles reside,
Even the rocks can't help but abide.
Nature's whispers bring antics anew,
In a world where the silly moments brew!

The Soft Murmur of Sprouts

Little sprouts peek from the dark, damp floor,
With giggles and winks, they wish to explore.
One said, "Hey, can you see my new hat?"
While others replied, "Oh, we're all a bit flat!"

The sun tickles them, making them sway,
"Let's have a party!" the daisies say.
Toadstools dance in their polka-dot shoes,
While earthworms pipe up with the latest news.

A breeze tries to tell a funny tale,
But stumbles over a twig, it's on sale!
Each plant chuckles, spread wide their leaves,
As they share their stories that nature weaves.

In the tiny patch where they all convene,
The humor grows thick, a glorious green.
Sprouts and giggles fill the air so bright,
In this murmur, laughter feels just right!

Whispers of the Earth

In the mud, the worms plot a great escape,
Wiggling and giggling, they form a landscape.
They say, "Let's dance, we're not so shy!"
While the soil beneath gives a hearty sigh.

The rocks debate who's the best role model,
While puddles ponder their next big throttle.
A flower declares it's a fashion show,
As petals swap colors in radiant glow.

A beetle rides on a leafy boat,
Daydreaming of goldfish and hoping to float.
All while the grass whispers secrets and sighs,
Making up stories about clouds in the skies.

In this world of whispers, jokes spread wide,
The earth has humor that fills us with pride.
So pause and listen, you'll surely see,
Nature's giggles are the best company!

Fluttering Voices

In the park, two trees did chat,
One wore a hat, the other, a cat.
Frogs croaked back, they saw the scene,
Saying, 'Get along! You're too obscene!'

Squirrels laughed from branches high,
'Oh, the things you hear when you're shy!'
They whispered secrets to the breeze,
While bees buzzed on with such great ease.

The Language of the Trees

A birch told tales of a lost sock,
While oaks just chuckled, they had the clock.
Pine scents lingered in the air,
Chortling softly, they'd share a scare.

'What do you mean it's time to grow?'
'Can't we just groove, take it slow?'
With each clap of the fluttering limb,
They spun ideas, a whimsical hymn.

Songs of the Swaying Branches

The branches swayed to a funky beat,
While twigs did tap dance on green-edged seat.
Below, a rabbit, with rhythm, did prance,
Jiving to branches in silly advance.

A woodpecker joined, pecking in tune,
'Let's have a party! We'll go till noon!'
Dangling leaves wore party hats,
Cheering and clapping, imagining spats.

Gentle Breezes

A gentle breeze, oh so spry,
Tickled the leaves, making them sigh.
'Is it just me or is that a joke?'
Cackled a leaf, as laughter awoke.

'What did one twig say to the sun?'
'Can't wait for summer, let's have some fun!'
The breeze just giggled, teasing the bark,
'You're all just branches with dreams that spark!'

Soft Confessions

Two leaves confessed in a rustling hush,
'Think we have style, or just a big crush?'
They plotted a dance, what a sight to see,
Pollen arrived, with a wink, 'Join me!'

'From up here, the world is a jest,'
Said one cheeky leaf all dressed in zest.
So they twirled and whisked, under skies so blue,
Frolicking softly in nature's hue.

The Lament of the Forest Floor

Oh, the things I see below,
A critter's sock, a lost bow,
A fungus dancing, what a show,
While squirrels complain in the meadow.

Amidst the roots, a party starts,
With ants performing tiny arts,
A beetle plays some funny parts,
While mice doodle on their charts.

A dandelion claims its space,
Telling the wind with a funny face,
It trips on grass in a silly race,
And giggles, oh what a clumsy grace.

"Let's spin!" cries a brave little sprout,
While thorns shout loud in a pout,
But laughter's louder, no doubt,
As nature gives a joyful shout!

Wistful Breezes

The breeze comes laughing through the trees,
Tickling branches, rolling leaves,
It whispers secrets, here it weaves,
Jokes so silly, nature believes.

A bird swoops down with a corny line,
"Why did the twig cross that vine?"
"Because it wanted some sunshine!"
The forest chuckles, feeling fine.

From one tall trunk to the next,
The whispers share with no pretext,
"Why did the oak feel so perplexed?"
"Because it's stumped! What's coming next?"

A breeze that spins and twirls around,
With laughter echoing, all around,
Nature's comedy in every sound,
Making merry, as life's unbound!

Enigmatic Echoes

In shadows deep, a secret hum,
With squirrels chattering, having fun,
They plot and plan till the day is done,
In the echo chamber, under the sun.

"Knock-knock!" calls the wise old owl,
"Who's there?" echoes, and they growl,
"Leafy Larry with a big scowl!"
Nature's giggle sounds like a growl.

As whispers bounce off rocks and trees,
Lingering lightly with the breeze,
"Did you hear the one about the bees?"
"They buzz around like they know ease!"

The forest wide bursts out a cheer,
Echoes of laughter far and near,
A riddle here, a joke to share,
The woods alive, with love and flair!

The Gentle Touch of Nature

With every step, the ground will chuckle,
Beneath our feet, it likes to buckle,
A silly dance that makes us struggle,
While whispers giggle and words all snuggle.

The flowers bloom, but what do they say?
"Hey, butterfly, don't fly away!"
They chat about the sunny day,
Though ants just wish to get some hay.

In playful pranks, the breeze persists,
Tickling leaves with tiny twists,
"Catch me if you can," it insists,
While branches sway, their moods are mixed!

Nature's tickle, from skies to ground,
Where every laugh is lost, then found,
With joy and quirks all flying 'round,
In gentle touches, laughter drowned!

Whispers of the Woods

In the forest so deep, critters sing,
Squirrels trade jokes about winter's fling.
Birds chirp punchlines in high-pitched tones,
While trees chuckle softly, creaking their bones.

A raccoon in shades claims he's a star,
He moonwalks along like a true avatar.
The chipmunks agree, they all clap their paws,
As the mushrooms giggle, holding in their flaws.

Branches sway left, branches sway right,
Telling tall tales under the soft moonlight.
Each leaf a witness to laughter's spree,
Nature's own comedy show, wild and free.

Even the owls are snickering low,
With wisdom wrapped in a feathery glow.
They hoot out riddles that leave us in glee,
As laughter spills forth, from each bough and tree.

Sylvan Stories

Underneath the boughs, a party unfolds,
Where acorns tell secrets, and stories are bold.
The ferns dance around, like they're at a ball,
Spinning and twirling until the leaves fall.

A fox wearing glasses reads tales with flair,
While rabbits in tuxes lounge without care.
The wind plays DJ, spinning tunes on repeat,
As critters groove by, in their furry little feet.

The beavers are builders of grand comedy sets,
Constructing great scenes with logs and offsets.
They crack up the crowd with well-timed gags,
As owls drop in, wearing party tags.

Amidst all the laughter, a tree snaps its trunk,
Critiquing the jokes, with a grunt and a funk.
But in this wood, filled with giggles and roars,
There's always a place for fun and more scores.

Murmuring Memories

Once a twig told a tale, long and winding,
About the summers spent cold drink-finding.
The thorns laughed loud, as petals turned red,
Recalling the pranks that the roots would spread.

Old stones reminisce of a frog's croaking song,
Chasing off shadows that didn't belong.
With laughter like bubbles, they float through the air,
Unraveling jokes with a whimsical flair.

The crickets are masters of late-night stand-up,
Buzzing their tales in a clumsy old cup.
While beetles applaud, doing tiny cartwheels,
All under the watch of the moon's spinning wheels.

In the woods where the laughter echoes so clear,
The past hums a melody, full of good cheer.
With each rustle and sway, there's a punchline to trace,
As memories giggle, leaving smiles on each face.

Resonance of the Trees

In the orchard, the branches sway and tease,
Tickling the squirrels, oh how they wheeze!
Every nut that drops is a laugh that flies,
As the bumblebees buzz with their embarrass'd sighs.

The pines are philosophers, wise but absurd,
Spouting quips louder than any of heard.
With cones full of humor, they tumble and roll,
While the mushrooms snort laughter, losing control.

Ladybugs flutter with tales of their tails,
Swapping wild stories of wind and of gales.
"No bug could catch me!" the dragonflies boast,
As they dive to the ground without fear or a host.

In this realm where nature holds its own flair,
Every rustling leaf has a joke to share.
The comedy flows as the trees sway and lean,
In this funny old forest, where laughter is seen.

Soft Words on the Autumn Air

As the breezes begin to tease,
Whispers dance among the trees.
A squirrel laughs, it's quite a sight,
Chasing acorns left and right.

The branches share their funny tales,
Of lost hats and gusty gales.
A chipmunk giggles with delight,
In a leaf pile, what a plight!

Leaves flutter down like gentle jokes,
Tickling noses of curious folks.
Each gust a pun, a playful jab,
"Oh dear me, that's quite the blab!"

In autumn's charm, we find our cheer,
Nature's laughter loud and clear.
So let the air be light and fun,
For nature's whispers have begun.

Twilit Tidings in the Woodland

As dusk descends, the shadows stretch,
The trees might giggle, then they fetch.
A rabbit hops in fancy shoes,
With tiny pants, it prances loose.

"Oh dear," sighs Owl, "What a show!
The moon's our spotlight, don't you know?"
The crickets chirp a lively tune,
While fireflies dance, oh what a boon!

Mice in jackets waltz in pairs,
While raccoons do their acrobat stares.
The twilit woodland, filled with glee,
A wacky ball, just wait and see!

Twilight giggles, nature's jest,
With woodland sprites, all feel blessed.
So come and join in, take a chance,
Leave worries behind, let's all dance!

Rustling Secrets

In every rustle, secrets hide,
A beetle's gossip, squirrel's pride.
"Oh look!" a twig shouts with a crack,
"Guess who's coming? It's that quack!"

The leaves gossip, shifting shades,
"Did you hear? Tim's new charades!"
A dance-off planned beneath the sun,
Where woodland creatures laugh and run.

Each breeze brings news, a playful tease,
Of sleepy hedgehogs and ladybees.
"I lost a sock!" a badger cries,
While hedgehogs roll, in such surprise!

With rustling giggles, the day drifts slow,
As secrets swirl like leaves in tow.
Join in the fun, let laughter sing,
In nature's world, we're all a king!

Echoes of Grace

In the forest, echoes leap,
Where playful shadows start to creep.
"Did you hear?" a crow takes flight,
"Today's the day we prank the night!"

With graceful sways, the branches nod,
As they plot mischief, feeling odd.
A raccoon moons us from a tree,
"Care to join my folly spree?"

The sun dips low, the giggles grow,
"Quick! Hide the snacks! Here comes the show!"
The giggling leaves set quite a pace,
In chaos, there's such funny grace!

So let the echoes call you near,
In this wild wood, there's much to cheer.
With every laugh, the daylight fades,
Just come along, and share the shades!

Soft Footfalls of Nature

In the woods, a squirrel stumbles,
With acorns flying, oh what fumbles!
A chipmunk laughs, it can't believe,
Nature's dance, a comic tease.

A deer slips by on clumsy hooves,
Trip over roots, it barely moves!
The rabbits chuckle, "You need a map!"
As nature giggles in joyful clap.

The birds are chirping silly songs,
A mock debate on who belongs.
A crow caws loud with such a flair,
"Who wore it best? The fox or hare?"

The sun peeks in with a mischievous eye,
Painting scenes where chimps can fly.
A game of hide-and-seek unfolds,
In the woods where laughter delights and holds.

Hushed Conversations

Beneath the boughs, the whispers flow,
A snail complains, "It's way too slow!"
A frog quips back, "At least you're sly,
You never worry when rains come by!"

A wise old owl, perched on a limb,
Says, "Hey fellas, let's not be dim!
Life's a joke, let's make it grand,
With silly pranks and laughter planned."

The raccoons plot a midnight feast,
"Steal the picnic? Oh, what a beast!"
But the humans laugh, they know it well,
They've hidden goodies, all's fair in this spell!

And when the moon's a silver gleam,
Nature grins, it's all a dream.
Dancing shadows, echoing calls,
In the enchanted woods where laughter falls.

Nature's Gentle Susurration

Amid the grass, the crickets sing,
A tune so funny, it's a swing!
The fireflies wink, "We steal the show,
With dazzling lights, we steal the glow!"

The ants parade in single file,
One trips and falls—it's worth the while!
They laugh it off, "It's just a slip,
We'll blame the leaves—they're on a trip!"

In cozy nooks, the hedgehogs cheer,
"Let's roll and tumble; it's time for beer!"
With acorn caps as makeshift cups,
They toast to joy and silly ups!

As leaves engage in playful waltz,
The breeze lets out a chuckle, halts.
For nature's pulse, both near and far,
Is woven fun, our lucky star!

Caresses of the Forest

Rustling branches make a scene,
"Did you see that? A squirrel's queen!"
With twigs and leaves, she struts around,
A crown of acorns in her crown.

The bunnies gather, placing bets,
"Will she make it? No more threats!"
They giggle soft, a hoppy cheer,
As twinkling stars begin to peer.

The wind plays tricks, it blows a kiss,
It ruffles feathers, what pure bliss!
The creatures join in, a merry throng,
In a forest anthem, a nonsense song.

So if you wander where trails weave,
Listen closely and you might believe,
That nature speaks with cheeky grace,
In a world where laughter finds its place.

Veiled Conversations under the Sky

In the park, two trees conspire,
Swaying gently, their leaves retire.
They giggle softly, sharing a jest,
While passersby think they're just rest.

A squirrel scurries, thinking he's wise,
Eavesdropping on those leafy lies.
"Did you hear what the birch said?
I can't believe she's lost her thread!"

The branches sway, a laughter low,
As birds join in, putting on a show.
They bob and weave, acting the fool,
While the sunlight turns them into gold.

With the moon now peeking, it's time for flaps,
The leaves make jokes about the fat chaps.
"Oh look! That's just a bundle of fluff,
When did he think he'd gotten enough?"

Tales Carried on Soft Winds

A gust whispers secrets, oh what a tease,
Tales of a chipmunk who tried to sneeze.
His tiny friends giggle under the shade,
While he claims he was totally unafraid.

Dandelions dance, with wishes so bold,
"Let's hope that was not what I foretold!"
The wind just chuckles, a merry old pal,
As petals tumble, making quite the gal.

The willows snicker, swaying side to side,
As crickets join in, their chirps amplified.
"Why did the acorn go to the ball?
To show off his cap and have a great fall!"

A breeze tickles toes as night falls in cheer,
With tales that restore what's lost with the year.
In this laughter, they find solace and play,
As stories unspool till the end of the day.

The Quiet Chorus of the Grove

In a grove where giggles softly collide,
The leaves all whisper in rhythmic stride.
"Why did the tree break up with the vine?
She said their connection was too intertwined!"

Amidst the branches, shadows take turns,
Each flicker of light, a giggle that churns.
The ferns are shaking, can't keep a straight face,
As beetles make jokes of their timeless race.

A banter erupts, with frogs in the lead,
"Ribbit, I heard he'll dance with a seed!"
And laughter cascades like rain from above,
The chorus of green, their antics we love.

When the sun sets low and the stars peek through,
The jokes grow taller, old friendships renew.
In this woody realm, with humor's embrace,
It's a whimsical night in a verdant space.

Whispers in the Twilight

As twilight falls, the fireflies gleam,
The trees conspire, weaving a dream.
"Did you hear what the oak tried to prove?
He thought he could breakdance, but couldn't move!"

The shadows stretch, in a playful way,
While rabbits debate on who won the race.
"Don't ask the hedgehog, he's quite a bore,
He just tells stories of battles of yore!"

In the distance, a hoot of an owl,
Takes in the banter with a knowing scowl.
"Leave them to giggle, they're far too loud,
For wisdom is quiet, not part of the crowd."

But laughter persists through each rustling leaf,
As dusk cultivates joy, beyond the belief.
With humor in echoes, and voices alive,
In this twilight setting, the spirit will thrive.

Verdant Parables

In a grove where giggles thrive,
The trees tell jokes to stay alive.
A squirrel rolls by, so full of glee,
"I'm not a nut! I'm just a tree!"

Beneath the shade, a chicken clucks,
"I've got the best of forest luck!"
But Freddy Frog takes quite a leap,
"Your dance is good, but mine's a sweep!"

And in the branches, owls convene,
Arguing if toast is truly green.
"I like it jellied, nice and spread!"
"Now you're just talking out your head!"

When breezes blow, they break the trance,
The trees sway to their laughter dance.
With every gust, the fun returns,
In the forest, joy just burns!

Breezy Conversations

A rustling sound, a leafy chat,
"Is it me, or is that a gnat?"
The oak says, "You complain too much,
Just take a sip, it's nature's touch!"

A willow hangs low, makes a face,
"I'm feeling quite out of place!"
"Don't pout!" shouts a nearby pine,
"With branches like yours, you'll be just fine!"

In a whirlwind, the gossip flows,
"Did you hear what the river knows?"
A breeze chuckles, "She's got a crush,
On the rock who makes her waters rush!"

The laughter peals, it fills the air,
With each soft flutter, we all share.
In nature's realm, humor survives,
Even trees have funny lives!

The Forest's Breath

Whispers swirl amongst the groves,
Where every tree wears leafy robes.
A chipmunk shouts, "I'll be a star!"
Then trips and lands with a loud, "RAR!"

The birch shakes its bark, quite amused,
"If you don't laugh, you'll be confused!"
But the pine just sways, so serenely,
"Indulge in joy, it's so cleanly!"

And down below, the rabbits hop,
Making mistakes that never stop.
"Left foot first! No, that's not right!"
"Now who's this clumsy in the night?"

Each gust brings tales from olden times,
In playful whims and quirky rhymes.
Nature's giggles roll and spread,
With every breath, fun is fed!

Shadows of the Past

In tangled roots, old stories spin,
Of what lay lost, where to begin?
A tortoise laughs, with a wink,
"I'm faster than most, don't you think?"

The ancient oak, with wisdom vast,
Whispers, "Youth, it always skips past!"
While young saplings barely stand tall,
"We're growing up, in laughter, we'll sprawl!"

Through dappled light, the shadows prance,
A dance of whimsy, a leaf's romance.
"What's your secret for a long life?"
"To pick up fun, and dodge the strife!"

With every clap of wind that blows,
The stories twist, the humor glows.
In the heart of woods, so vast and bright,
The shadows laugh, into the night!

Shadows Talking in the Wind

In the back yard, shadows play,
Chatting secrets, come what may.
They tell tales of missing socks,
And how squirrels stole their clocks.

A leaf giggles, 'Did you hear?
The cat just jumped, out of sheer fear!'
Breezes chuckle, swirling fast,
As shadows dance, a comical cast.

Grass blades gossip, waving too,
'That jaybird thinks he's quite the crew!'
While flowers snicker at the fuss,
Bouncing lightly, all nonplussed.

Under the sun, the fun won't cease,
Each laugh a tickle, feathered fleece.
They plot pranks on passersby,
'Next time, let's steal the pie!'

Thrum of Nature's Narrative

In the woods, a tale unfolds,
Where chatter's vivid, mischief bold.
The river brags of fish it caught,
And missed the boat — or so it thought!

Trees gossip in rustling tones,
'Why did that guy drop his phones?'
A beetle bursts with hearty cheer,
'Just keep rolling — don't you fear!'

A butterfly swoops down and twirls,
'Last week's wind? It gave me swirls!'
Caterpillars laugh, oh what a show,
'Can you believe how slow we grow?'

Each petal's grin blooms just for fun,
While crickets chirp, 'Come join the run!'
Together they craft a comic spree,
Nature's tale, wild and free!

Whispers of the Wandering Woods

In the bushes, whispers blend,
Squirrels plotting tricks they'll send.
Shuffling leaves with quips so sly,
'Watch out for that sneaky pie!'

Footsteps crunch — a deer scoffs loud,
'Is that a human in the crowd?'
The dandelions, so full of sass,
Call out, 'Hey, stop cutting grass!'

Beneath the branches, laughter swells,
As mushrooms shape into tiny gels.
They bounce and jiggle on the ground,
While acorns roll, oh what a sound!

Gusts arrive with giggles bright,
Swooshing by in pure delight.
Together they sing a joyous cheer,
Where friendships bloom from ear to ear!

The Lullaby of Swirling Foliage

In the glade, a soft song plays,
Leaves twirling in whimsical ways.
A frog croaks jokes, so funny and light,
While crickets chirp, 'What a sight!'

With leaves that jiggle, the wind sets forth,
'Did you hear about our new turf?'
The sunbeams twinkle in golden frames,
As every branch joins in the games.

Vines wiggle, sharing playful tease,
'Let's trip the cat — oh, if you please!'
The whispers grow, a caper brewed,
Echoing joyous, carefree mood.

The night descends, yet laughter soars,
Through moonlit tales, nature roars.
In every rustle, joy prevails,
A whisper of life in merry trails!

Midnight Serenade of Foliage

Under the canopy, shadows prance,
Naughty branches in a leafy dance,
A squirrel giggles at the moon's bright stare,
Whiskers twitch, he's lost without a care.

Crickets join in, a concert so grand,
Waving their bows, each tiny hand,
They play their tunes with zest and glee,
While frogs croak bass, as low as can be.

An owl hoots, "Hey, keep it down!"
As raccoons shout, "We're the best in town!"
A leaf drops low, it took a bow,
Applause erupts, "Let's take a vow!"

In this silly night, let laughter reign,
Nature's jesters free of all their pain,
Upon this stage where shadows live,
Let joy be the song that nature gives!

Tales Woven in Green

Once upon a fern, a frog told a tale,
Of a mouse and a cat, who set off to sail,
They traveled on grass blades, oh, what a ride,
While the wind made sure they were nothing to hide.

A hedgehog chimed in, "Whoa, I want to steer!"
With a twitch of his nose, he took off with cheer,
The others all chuckled, a hapless crew,
As they zigged and zagged in this green avenue.

A dragonfly buzzed, "Hey, let's play a game!"
And soon every critter was calling a name,
"Spin the acorn, it's a top-notch spree!"
While leaves fell around them, as happy as can be.

The sun began to set, a curtain of gold,
The stories of old, by the night hours told,
With laughter and whispers, under moonbeam's sheen,
Tales come alive, in the forest so green!

The Language of Rustle

In the forest's tongue, the leaves all chat,
A tap dance of voices, imagine that!
With every breeze, a story is spun,
Nature's giggles, oh what fun!

"Hey there, twig!" a brave petal would say,
"Join our gossip, don't drift away,"
The bushes all shiver, with secrets to share,
While the wind spins them round, without a care.

A bark from a tree, "I'm wise like a sage!"
While the critters laugh, "You forgot your age!"
Yet every chuckle echoes, a symphony sweet,
Where rustles together create a funny beat.

As twilight wraps soft like a snug little quilt,
They weave tales of old, of mischief and guilt,
With a sip of moonlight, under stars up high,
These whispering giggles, let's never say bye!

Where Silence Meets Sound

Amidst sleepy woods, where night creeps near,
Hushed whispers flutter, tickling the ear,
Crickets serenade, a tune quite absurd,
While owls hoot back, "I haven't heard!"

A rustle from bushes, a prankster's delight,
A rabbit pops out—oh, what a sight!
He jumps and he jiggles, a dance so bright,
While shadows giggle, cloaked in the night.

"Let's start a party!" calls out a butterfly,
As fireflies twinkle, floating by and by,
They swirl in a circle, a jolly brigade,
Painting the darkness where laughter won't fade.

So when you wander, to places unknown,
Remember the jests that the twilight has sown,
For in every rustle, and silence profound,
Joy resides sweetly, where laughter is found!

Enchanted Cadences

In the forest, a squirrel prances,
Chasing shadows, doing funny dances.
The acorns giggle, they roll away,
While the trees chuckle at their play.

A raccoon juggles with shiny cans,
While birds critique his silly plans.
Laughter echoes through the twinkling light,
As critters unite to frolic all night.

Beneath the boughs, a party unfolds,
With tales of mischief, both daring and bold.
The breeze joins in with a playful tease,
Whispering secrets that rustle the leaves.

In this kingdom of humor and cheer,
Every rustling sound brings smiles near.
Nature's jesters, all in their prime,
Dance in rhythm, as if keeping time.

Echoing Embraces

The wind plays tag with a playful glee,
Tickling the branches, desperate to flee.
A wobbly cloud takes a dive for a laugh,
As grinning daisies plot their own autograph.

A porcupine dons a coat made of thorns,
While chipmunks scheme in mischievous adorns.
With every rustle, a giggle escapes,
As trees share the news of their fanciful capes.

Through tangled roots, the jokes intertwine,
Each vine a pun, wrapped up in sunshine.
The chorus of nature—a comical show,
Where each leaf chuckles with an audacious glow.

Laughter rings out, a melodious song,
In a world where the whimsical belong.
While echoes embrace both vibrant and spry,
The humor spins wide beneath the sky.

Leaves Like Lullabies

A breezy giggle turns into a whirl,
As leaves speak softly, twirl and swirl.
In a hammock of shadows, a frog does a flip,
While a wise old owl gives a comical quip.

Snails wear their shells like hats in a row,
While hoppers put on a leggy show.
The grass blades bend to hear every jest,
In this playful patch where all are blessed.

The moonlight shines with an innocent stare,
As fireflies blink and waltz in the air.
With a tinkle of laughter, the night takes flight,
In a lullaby whispered, through the fun-filled night.

Amidst the giggles, the world falls asleep,
While leaves share secrets they promise to keep.
The forest chuckles as shadows parade,
In a symphony where joy is displayed.

Between Sunlight and Shade

In the glimmering gaps, shadows softly play,
While whispers of fun guide the bright day.
A ladybug winks with a wink and a hop,
While cheeky little rabbits forget to stop.

The flowers flicker in a colorful trance,
Inviting the bees to join in the dance.
But one little gust sends a dandelion spun,
As seeds scatter far, oh what a fun run!

Squirrels chase tails in a blur of delight,
As butterflies banter in colorful flight.
The sunlight giggles as it paints the ground,
In a world where joy is profoundly found.

Between the rays, in shadows so keen,
Nature spins tales that remain unseen.
With every chuckle from the branches above,
The rhythm of life blossoms with love.

Gentle Voices of Flora

In gardens where the daisies chat,
A haughty rose once wore a hat.
The tulips giggled, oh so bright,
As bumblebees took off in flight.

The lilacs whispered silly jokes,
While daisies rolled with laughing folks.
A dandelion's wish left to fate,
As a squirrel danced, trying to be great.

The ferns waved arms like they were cool,
While trembling grass avoided school.
In the sun, the petals did prance,
Inviting all to join the dance!

Each flower has a funny story,
In colors bright, it shares the glory.
In this garden, joy does reign,
Where laughter flows like a sweet refrain.

Shadows of Whispered Dreams

In twilight's arms, the shadows play,
With crickets singing night away.
The moonlight draped on weary trees,
Allows the branches to crack such teas.

A fox once tried to tell a tale,
But tripped on roots and left a trail.
The hooting owl swooped down low,
To share some puns that stole the show.

A bat complained of being late,
To join the party at the gate.
While shadows danced with crazy glee,
In whispered dreams, they strung a spree.

The night held secrets, oh so sly,
Where fireflies blinked and dared to fly.
Filled with laughter, not a frown,
As dreams tumbled, shirts inside out.

The Tones of Tranquility

In soothing tones of nature's breath,
The chickadees sing of life and death.
They chirp about a worm so bold,
Who dreamt of gold but turned to mold.

A meadowlark burst into song,
As butterflies danced all day long.
With tunes so light, they floated high,
While ants debated who would fly.

The doves coo and make no sense,
While ladybugs debate defense.
Each note a chuckle from above,
Where laughter spills like a push and shove.

Together, they weave a merry sound,
In harmony where joy is found.
From tranquil woods to misty streams,
Life's a melody filled with dreams.

Hymns of the Woodland

In woods where squirrels barter nuts,
The tree trunks shake at their funny struts.
Each leaf is tuned to nature's call,
Where laughter lifts and carries all.

A bear once tried on a fancy hat,
While rabbits giggled, 'What's up with that?'
The chipmunks turned in tiny glee,
As they penned tales of best-of-three.

Mushrooms danced in the soft moonlight,
And raccoons debated 'who's most bright?'
Echoes filled with mirth and cheer,
Painting smiles to every ear.

From every branch, a joke is spun,
Where woodland creatures laugh and run.
In harmony, they sing their tunes,
Under the watchful gaze of moons.

www.ingramcontent.com/pod-product-compliance
Lightning Source LLC
Chambersburg PA
CBHW070332120526
44590CB00017B/2854